Trader Quotivation

Arranged by

Private Trading Coach

ISBN: 1523254580
ISBN-13: 978-1523254583

DEDICATION

To fellow traders around the globe.

May these quotations provide fuel
for your trading endeavors.

DISCLAIMER

Every reasonable effort has been made to ensure the accuracy and origins of the following quotations.

Any perceived or real misrepresentations are purely unintentional in nature and not meant to cause harm to any person or third party whatsoever.

Additionally, every reasonable effort has been made to rightfully attribute each quotation to the original author(s).

In some cases it was impossible to identify who first spoke or wrote a particular quotation, plus some quotations have several similar variations. To decide which specific quotation to use selections were made using the version from the author(s) most connected with the endeavor of trading.

FOREWARD

The pages ahead contain a fine selection of trading related quotations. They originate mainly from active traders but also the wider trading community too – past and present.

Many experienced traders will openly admit that even when they became consistently profitable there were still some psychologically impactful trading days. Such days might occur less frequently, or to a lesser extent. But, the bottom line is that everyone in the trading world requires sparks of motivation or wisdom from those who've gone before them – sometimes simply just to keep going.

So, keep this book close at hand, either on your trading desk or in your trading library. Hopefully you will call upon it again and again to find inspiration and motivation for your own trading journey.

TRADER QUOTIVATION

"If your goal is to be a pro trader, your question should
not be how much will you make this year.
Your question should be how to survive for 30 years."
- Peter L. Brandt

"Accepting losses is the most important single
investment device to insure safety of capital."
- Gerald M. Loeb

"Trading is more about knowing when not to trade
than it is about trading. Trading is timing.
Waiting is painful. Pain brings wisdom. Wisdom brings
balance. Trading can be excruciatingly exciting when done
wrong, and tauntingly tedious when done right."
- Jeff Cooper

"Have something in your life more
important than trading."
- Dr. Brett Steenbarger

"The best traders wake up every day excited.
They can't wait to get to work.
Passion transcends monetary reward."
- Mark Minervini

"Every time you make money trading,
it's like applause but only you hear it."
- Pete Najarian

"Know yourself and provide
against your own weakness."
- Edwin Lefèvre

"Trading the markets is living a few years like most people won't, so that you can spend the rest of your life like most people can't."
- Yvan Byeajee

"It [trading] took me years and years full time working at it, I thought it would take me a few months."
- Tim Rea

"Markets are repetitive. In its purest form this game is simply trading repetitive patterns. More experience you have the easier it becomes."
- Assad Tannous

"One of the things I have noticed among successful traders is that they are usually able to adapt to changing market conditions."
- Dr. Brett Steenbarger

"Saying all you need to trade successfully is a laptop is like saying all you need to run a world record 100m is a pair of legs."
- Tom Dante

"Money management makes all the difference."
- Thomas Stridsman

"At the stock exchange, two times two is never four, but five minus one. You just gotta have the nerve to accept and endure the minus one."
- A. Kostolany

"The more you think you know, the more closed-minded you'll be."
- Ray Dalio

"I always say you could publish [trading] rules in a
newspaper and no one would follow them."
- Richard Dennis

"As in roulette, same is true of the stock trader, who
will find that the expense of trading
weights the dice heavily against him."
- B. Graha

"Always discipline yourself by
following a pre-determined set of rules."
- Linda Bradford Raschke

"The more you understand the concept you are trading,
how it might behave under all sorts of market conditions,
the less historical testing you need to do."
- Tom Basso

"Fundamentalists that don't pay attention
to the charts are like a doctor who says he's
not going to take a patient's temperature."
- Bruce Kovner

"If you believe you or anyone else has a system to
predict the future of the market, the joke is on you."
- R. Wanger

"Most people get interested in stocks
when everyone else is.
The time to get interested is when no one else is."
- Warren Buffett

"Trend does not exist in the now and the phrase, 'the
trend' has no inherent meaning."
- Ed Seykota

"Keeping a journal is one of the first things mentors at trading firms will recommend to their apprentices. The journal is a great way of tracking what we do and why we do it."
- Dr. Brett Steenbarger

"Trading is only exciting when you are starting out. When you excel at it, it is as boring as it can be. Trust me."
- Henri M. Simoes

"Never commit more than five percent of your money to a single trade idea."
- Michael Marcus

"Any system will perform better under certain market conditions. Trend following systems do better when the markets are trending and quiet; countertrend systems do better when markets are stable and volatile."
- Curtis Faith

"If a man didn't make mistakes, he'd own the world in a month. But if he didn't profit by his mistakes he wouldn't own a blessed thing."
- Jesse Livermore

"I believe that the money I make in the markets is really made in the days, weeks, months before. It is the preparation for the trades."
- Rob Hanna

"Either a trade is good enough to take, in which case it should be implemented at full size, or it's not worth bothering with at all."
- William Eckhardt

"People can't predict markets
but markets can predict people."
- Rick Ferri

"Remember, your goal is to trade well,
not to trade often."
- Dr. Alexander Elder

"Understand that learning the markets can take years.
Immerse yourself in the world of trading
and give up everything else."
- Linda Bradford Raschke

"Don't speculate
unless you can make it a full-time job."
- Bernard Baruch

"Time and time again, I give traders
who work with me one piece of advice:
Do more of what works and less of what doesn't."
- Steve Clark

"Ultimately you don't trade the market,
you trade your personality."
- Larry Williams

"If you try to engineer all of the risk out of a trade, it
will only surface somewhere else when it is least welcome."
- Perry J. Kaufman

"Every trading system evolves. Once you stop evolving
a system [it is dead]. No system works forever."
- Mark B. Fisher

"You are the most important
variable in the trading equation."
- Mike Elvin

"Just because you've made money in the markets does
not mean you have an ounce of intelligence."
- Larry Williams

"If everyone was right and no one was wrong,
"everybody" would be rich
and nobody would be poor."
- Randolph Newman

"Watching the screen creates an urge to do something
and a sense of constantly missed opportunities."
- Gerald Appel

"Time is your friend; impulse is your enemy."
- John Bogle

"Without a trading system you are floating aimlessly in
a sea of opportunity with no land in sight."
- Mark Douglas

"Don't let yourself get overwhelmed
by the tough times. The losses.
The day to day grind of it.
Try to elevate a little bit above that…."
- Toby Crabel

"I have gathered enough experience
to realize that I can NEVER break my rules.
Not one trade can be the exception."
- Mark Crisp

"Your trading performance is a direct reflection of how
you feel internally, not the other way round.
When you feel good, you perform at high levels."
- Robert Koppel

"You can succeed in trading. It has been done before,
and it's being done right now, today,
by people who started from scratch."
- Dr. Alexander Elder

"First you learn the game, and then you learn you.
Without you, there is nothing:
no profits, no consistency and no dreams."
- Anand Sanghvi

"The game of speculation is the most uniformly
fascinating game in the world. But it is not a game for the
stupid, the mentally lazy, the person of inferior emotional
balance, or the get rich quick adventurer.
They will die poor."
- Jesse Livermore

"Most often, I'll get out if the market fails
to do what I expect it to do.
The best patterns give instant feedback."
- Linda Bradford Raschke

"At the end of the day, the most important thing is
how good are you at risk control."
- Paul Tudor Jones

"Trade quality, not quantity.
Take the best of the best.
Get the big picture."
- Joe Ross

"If nothing is threatening, there's nothing to fear."
- Mark Douglas

"Bakers make bread, cobblers make shoes,
traders make money."
- Anon

"You can't control what the market does, but you can
control your reaction to the market."
- Steve Cohen

"If you can't measure it, you probably can't manage
it…Things you measure tend to improve."
- Ed Seykota

"Whenever you find the key to the market;
they change the locks."
- Gerald M. Loeb

"The first principle is that you must not fool yourself,
and you are the easiest person to fool."
- Richard Feynman

"Human emotion is both the source of opportunity in
trading and the greatest challenge.
Master it and you will succeed."
- Curtis Faith

"The purpose of trading is to make money, but if you
focus too much on the money,
you'll end up shooting yourself in the foot."
- Yvan Byeajee

"Are you long because you are bullish
or bullish because you are long."
- Jim Paul

"Discipline comes from confidence, confidence comes from having [trading] methodologies that work."
- Jake Bernstein

"People hate to lose more than they love to win."
- Roy Niederhoffer

"Trade like you don't need the money.
It takes so much pressure off you."
- Martin Niemi

"A new trader probably can't handle the emotions that come with larger accounts and would likely trade emotions instead of their trading plan."
- Steve Burns

"Don't be a hero. Don't have an ego."
- Paul Tudor Jones

"A beginning trader must first learn how to lose in order to learn how to win.
Losing is primary a function of capital preservation."
- Peter L. Brandt

"The key [to trading] is consistency and discipline."
- Richard Dennis

"You can line up more experts than you can shake a stick at, but none can predict with certainty what investors really want to know:
How will the market do tomorrow,
or next week, or next year?"
- John Neff

"The best cure for low prices is low prices."
- Emma O'Brien

"I see the younger generation hampered
by the need to understand and rationalize why
something should go up or down.
Usually, by the time that becomes self-evident,
the move is already over."
- Paul Tudor Jones

"A hallmark of great traders is
the ability to do ordinary things consistently
which in turn produce extraordinary results."
- Assad Tannous

"It's not the money that brings them [independent
traders] happiness but rather the time and independence."
- Brady Dahl

"Probably 80% of your profits are going
to come from 10% of your trades."
- Linda Bradford Raschke

"Good trading is boring. Gamblers seek excitement,
pros seek consistent profitability and low volatility.
That is how longevity is achieved."
- Mark Minervini

"I try my hardest to break even psychologically
after every trade and every day."
- Anon

"No matter how good a trader you think you are,
the markets are always going to screw with your head
and test your mental fortitude."
- Mark B. Fisher

"Psychologically, most of us prefer
comfort and safety to risk taking."
- Ari Kiev

"Every once in a while go to cash, take a break.
Don't try to play the market all the time.
Too tough on the emotions."
- Jesse Livermore

"The more sophisticated you become as a trader, the
more you will realize that trading is completely mental."
- Mark Douglas

"There are two kinds of people that lose money; those
that know nothing and those that know everything."
- R. Lenzner

"It should be noted that, though I have made extensive
use of statistics, my focus is not on the rigorous
application of statistical methods."
- Toby Crabel

"The skills we are taught that should carry us through
life, turn out to be inappropriate for trading."
- Thom Hartle

"To be a winning trader, you have to be among the
best. There can be no middle ground."
- Joe Ross

"Understand your limitations.
Everyone has limitations, even the best traders."
- Mark Weinstein

"If you personalize losses, you can't trade."
- Bruce Kovner

"What would make my trading day a success today,
even if I don't make money?"
- Dr. Brett Steenbarger

"My mission has always been
to help people transform for the better;
I just happen to do it through a trading metaphor."
- Dr. Van Tharp

"The truth was that as my pocket had strengthened, my
head had weakened. I became over-confident..."
- Nicolas Darvos

"Stress is literally kryptonite to traders. Stress disrupts
their equilibrium and affects their decision-making."
- Gatis Roze

"The investor's chief problem, and even his worst
enemy, is likely to be himself."
- Benjamin Graham

"In my world, I know you don't have to like it,
you just have to do it. That means I must continue
following a system...."
- Larry Williams

"Traders with the golden touch
do no talk about their success."
- Linda Bradford Raschke

"I truly believe if the majority of traders had unlimited
capital they would prove a lot more profitable, just because
of the sense of security it brings."
- Lawrie Inman

"No profession requires more hard work,
intelligence, patience, and mental discipline
than successful speculation."
- Robert Rhea

"Trading forces someone to think hard;
those who merely work hard generally lose
their focus and intellectual energy."
- Nassim N. Taleb

"For the successful trader knows
every action he takes, every decision he makes,
he and only he is responsible for that action."
- Mark Crisp

"[In trading] take home runs when you can, but don't
beat yourself up about missing a few."
- Vadym Graifer & Christopher Schumacher

"To be a super-trader, you'll need an edge
to overcome the laws of probability."
- Ari Kiev

"This ain't clipping coupons.
No risk, no return."
- Anon

"Nobody can give me a tip or series of tips that will
make more money for me than my own judgement."
- Jesse Livermore

"It is not the system that makes the trader, it is the
trader that makes the system."
- Scott Billington

"Getting into a trade is like jumping
into a fast-moving river.
The opportunity as well as the
danger is in the water."
- Dr. Alexander Elder

"A great trader is like a great athlete.
You have to have natural skills, but you have to train
yourself how to use them."
- Marty Schwartz

"The consistency you seek is
in your mind not in the markets."
- Mark Douglas

"Drawdowns in real life always seem to feel longer and
induce more pain than you'd imagine when looking back."
- Cliff Asness

"People just don't want to believe that anyone can
break away from the crowd and rise above mediocrity."
- Paul Tudor Jones

"Experienced traders control risk,
inexperienced traders chase gains."
- Alan Farley

"To be a money master,
you must first be a self-master."
- J.P. Morgan

"If there's one thing the great traders have in common.
It's they trade the same high probability pattern
over and over again."
- Assad Tannous

"At the end of the day,
I am a slave to the tape and proud of it."
- Paul Tudor Jones

"I'll keep reducing my trading size as long as I am
losing…. My money management techniques are extremely
conservative. I never risk anything approaching the total
amount of money in my account, let alone my total funds."
- Randy McKay

"You can only get good at trading if you love it."
- Steve Burns

"I have learned through the years that after a good run
of profits in the markets, it's very important
to take a few days off as a reward.
The natural tendency is to keep pushing until the streak
ends. But experience has taught me that a rest in the
middle of the streak can often extend it."
- Marty Schwartz

"A lagging indicator is something that tells you what is
going to happen after it already happened."
- Coreen T. Sol

"Unfortunately, most aspiring traders find out far too
late that the act of trading is
20% intellectual and 80% psychological."
- Michael Martin

"A trader needs to be very comfortable with himself
psychologically. He needs to be driving toward an
understanding of his strengths and weaknesses and his
attitude towards risk, frustration, money and wealth."
- Adam H. Grimes

"Successful trading is always an emotional battle for the speculator, not an intelligent battle."
- Jesse Livermore

"Discipline in trading means doing what you should do rather than what you want to do."
- Yvan Byeajee

"Never ask a trader if he is profitable, you can see it in his gesture and gait."
- Nassim N. Taleb

"There is no 'could have,' 'would have,' or 'should have' in trading."
- Anon

"Conditions are always imperfect!
You must allow yourself to fail.
Allow for human limitations and incorrect choices."
- Linda Bradford Raschke

"The key to trading success is emotional discipline."
- Victor Sperandeo

"The purpose of my research is to determine tradable market tendencies."
- Toby Crabel

"If you want to be successful, you need to think of the long run, and ignore the outcome of individual trades."
- Curtis Faith

"Please believe me when I say that behavior modification, is without doubt, the key to you trading success."
- Joe Ross

"If you don't have the patience [in trading] to wait, there will be nothing to wait for."
- Larry Williams

"If you don't know who you are, this [trading] is an expensive place to find out."
- George Goodman

"By worrying too much about how much money they make, traders can no longer follow markets with a clear head."
- Dr. Brett Steenbarger

"If you're not afraid [in trading] then you don't need courage."
- Mark Douglas

"The closer you sit to the screen, the more the issues of emotion and psychology come into the game."
- Gerald Appel

"I'd rather take a good trade that loses money than a bad trade that makes.
Good trades pay off over time. Bad trades kill you."
- Joel Kruger

"The goal of a successful trader is to make the best trades. Money is secondary."
- Dr. Alexander Elder

"Most trading edges are very small, so you must execute the trades flawlessly or you can turn a winning system into a losing one."
- Henri M. Simoes

"Successful traders isolate themselves
from the opinions of others."
- Linda Bradford Raschke

"There is time to go long, time to go short,
and a time to go fishing."
- Jesse Livermore

"If your edge puts the odds in your favor, then every
loss puts you that much closer to a win."
- Mark Douglas

"No matter how long you trade,
you'll never do it perfectly."
- Larry Williams

"You can limit your stress level by removing as many
unknowns as possible from your trading."
- Steve Burns

"Look for the trading method that's right for you, it's
not going to be the same for everybody."
- Jack Schwager

"By living the philosophy that winners are always in
front of me, it's not so painful to take a loss.
If I make a mistake so what!"
-Tom Baldwin

"Developing a trading system that works
is the easy part. Getting into the right mindset to apply
it is where most traders fail."
- Assad Tannous

"Emotions are your worst enemy in the stock market."
- Don Hays

"Leave your ego, emotions and bravado outside the
door of your trading room."
- Anon

"Don't let the outcome of one trade alter your trading
discipline. One trade doesn't make a system."
- Vadym Graifer & Christopher Schumacher

"Fortune tellers live in the future. So do people who
want to put things off. So do fundamentalists."
- Ed Seykota

"You are the most important element
in the equation for [trading] success."
- Linda Bradford Raschke

"There are no runners-up in trading,
you either get the gold or you give the gold."
- Joe Ross

"A lot of people get so enmeshed in the markets that
they lose their perspective."
- Marty Schwartz

"Being a consistent stock market winner
[in terms of effort] is no different from being a top
lawyer, doctor or businessman."
- Mark Crisp

"Have a plan and stick with it.
That works in trading, as well as in life."
- Mark B. Fisher

"If you really believe in random distribution between
wins and losses, can you ever feel betrayed by the market?"
- Mark Douglas

"These words [bullish, bearish] are not in my
vocabulary because I believe they can
create an emotional mind-set of a specific market
direction in a speculators mind."
- Jesse Livermore

"Almost anybody can make up a list of rules that are
80% as good as what we taught. What they can't do is give
[people] the confidence to stick to those rules
even when things are going bad."
- Richard Dennis

"Motivation is very important, especially early on.
Remember why you wanted to be a trader,
what it is you wanted to achieve."
- S. Hampton

"You only need one [trading] set-up to make a living."
- Linda Bradford Raschke

"[Trading] can change the station of an individual of
moderate income to one of financial independence."
- Ralph Ainsworth

"You have to figure out how to make money being
right only 20 to 30 percent of the time."
- Bill Lipschutz

"Lose your opinion, not your money."
- Linda Bradford Raschke

"Trade with an edge, manage risk,
be consistent, and keep it simple."
- Curtis Faith

"View each trade merely one
in a series of probabilities."
- Scott Billington

"You have to protect your nerves
and your capital as a trader."
- Steve Burns

"What screws us up most as traders is the picture we
hold in our head of how trading is supposed to be."
- Yvan Byeajee

"Trading a system that exerts the least amount of
emotional capital makes the
process of controlling emotions easier."
- Assad Tannous

"When you have a destabilizing loss, get out,
go home, take a nap, put a little time
between that and your next decision."
- Richard Dennis

"A trading career is a marathon, not a sprint: the
winners pace themselves."
- Dr. Brett Steenbarger

"I have been trading for decades and I am still
standing. I have seen a lot of traders come and go. They
have a system or a program that works in some specific
environments and fails in others. In contrast, my strategy is
dynamic and ever evolving. I constantly learn and change."
- Thomas Busby

"Speculation is not bad,
but bad speculation is a disaster."
- Larry Williams

"Amateur traders lose money
because they try to avoid losing.
Professional traders understand they
need to take losses to win."
- Jack Schwager

"I have a Ph.D in mathematics and a background in
cybernetics, but I was able to overcome those
disadvantages and make money [in trading]."
- Brian Monieson

"Assuming risk brings uncertainty, anxiety, and
occasional loss, but it also brings out the best in us."
- Victor Niederhoffer

"Successful trading is difficult and frustrating."
- Linda Bradford Raschke

"You adapt, evolve, compete or die [in trading]."
- Paul Tudor Jones

"The only difference between winners and losers
is that winners make small mistakes,
while losers make big mistakes."
- Ned Davis

"You control how you trade, the markets control how
and when you'll get paid."
Dr. Brett Steenbarger

"The market doesn't care where you went to school,
who your father is or isn't,
what country club you belong to...."
- Mike Bellafiore

"There is something magical about how the market
reinforces much deeper, existential truths..."
- Anand Sanghvi

"Trading is 24/7 for the first two years at least
- and then you can get some balance."
- Lex van Dam

"Not only is risk necessary for gain; it is the
inescapable lot of human beings."
- Victor Niederhoffer

"Make something constructive
come out of any trading loss."
- Yvan Byeajee

"The second, or last line of defense [against
committing a trading error] is to catch yourself in the act."
- Mark Douglas

"Overtrading suckers one into seeing only
the trees and missing the forest."
- Linda Bradford Raschke

"Most of the top traders have a life outside trading.
Realizing the importance of keeping it all in balance."
- Mark Crisp

"Once you have a [trading] system,
the biggest obstacle is trusting it."
- Tom Wills

"Trading is very competitive and you have to be able to
handle getting your butt kicked."
- Paul Tudor Jones

"Assimilate into your very bones
a set of trading rules that works for you."
- Linda Bradford Raschke

"[With trading] People want to stand at the top of the
mountain but they don't want to pack the gear,
prep for years and then endure the climb."
- Tom Dante

"You don't need to know what's going to happen next
to make money on that trade."
- Mark Douglas

"Discipline is a key element of successful trading,
nothing works in trading without the ability to take the
right action at the right time."
- Steve Burns

"Whatever you think it takes
to be a successful trader, multiple it by ten."
- Assad Tannous

"The relation between stock market and economy
is like a man walking his dog.
The man walks slowly, the dog runs back and forth."
- A. Kostolany

"Mentally strong traders embrace
change and fear stagnation."
- Joe Carapinha

"You can't expect to become a doctor or an attorney
overnight, and trading is no different."
- Mark Cook

"Mature understanding of and respect of risk is the
hallmark of the best traders."
- Curtis Faith

"First of all, never play macho man with the market.
Second, never overtrade."
- Paul Tudor Jones

"You must focus on being the best on a single trading
setup. Study the markets, study yourself
and find a trading edge that suits you."
- Henri M. Simoes

"My satisfaction always came from beating the market,
solving the puzzle. The money was the reward, but it was
not the main reason I loved the market."
- Jesse Livermore

"I know where I'm getting out before I get in."
- Bruce Kovner

TRADER QUOTIVATION

TRADER QUOTIVATION

TRADER QUOTIVATION

www.ingramcontent.com/pod-product-compliance
Lightning Source LLC
Chambersburg PA
CBHW070719210526
45170CB00021B/1240